THE ULTIMATE COFFE RECIPES COOKBOOK IN LESS THAN 5 MINUTES

100 COFFEE AND ESPRESSO HOMEMADE RECIPES THAT TASTE EXACTLY LIKE BAR!

RICHARD MURPHY

All rights reserved.

Disclaimer

The information contained in this eBook is meant to serve as a comprehensive collection of strategies that the author of this eBook has done research about. Summaries, strategies, tips and tricks are only recommendation by the author, and reading this eBook will not guarantee that one's results will exactly mirror the author's results. The author of the eBook has made all reasonable effort to provide current and accurate information for the readers of the eBook. The author and its associates will not be held liable for any unintentional error or omissions that may be found. The material in the eBook may include information by third parties. Third party materials comprise of opinions expressed by their owners. As such, the author of the eBook does not assume responsibility or liability for any third party material or opinions. Whether because of the progression of the internet, or the unforeseen changes in company policy and editorial submission guidelines, what is stated as fact at the time of this writing may become outdated or inapplicable later.

The eBook is copyright © 2022 with all rights reserved. It is illegal to redistribute, copy, or create derivative work from this eBook whole or in part. No parts of this report may be reproduced or retransmitted in any reproduced or retransmitted in any forms whatsoever without the writing expressed and signed permission from the author.

TABLE OF CONTENTS

TABLE OF CONTENTS4
INTRODUCTION8
ICED COFFEE10

1. ICED MOCHACCHINO11
2. ALMOND ICED COFFEE13
3. ICED CINNAMON COFFEE15
4. COFFEE ICE17
5. ICED CAFE AU LAIT19
6. CREAMY ICED COFFEE21
7. ICED SPICED COFFEE23

ALCOHOL-INFUSED COFFEE26

8. RUM COFFEE27
9. KAHLUA IRISH COFFEE29
10. BAILEY'S IRISH CAPPUCCINO31
11. BRANDY COFFEE33
12. KAHLUA AND CHOCOLATE SAUCE35
13. HOMEMADE COFFEE LIQUEUR37
14. KAHLUA BRANDY COFFEE39
15. LIME TEQUILA ESPRESSO41
16. SWEETENED BRANDY COFFEE43
17. DINNER PARTY COFFEE45
18. SWEET MAPLE COFFEE47
19. DUBLIN DREAM49
20. DI SARONNO COFFEE51
21. BAJA COFFEE53
22. PRALINE COFFEE55
23. PRALINE LIQUEUR57

24. Amaretto Cafe' 59
25. Cafe Au Cin 61
26. Spiked Cappuccino 63
27. Gaelic Coffee 65
28. Canadian Coffee 67
29. German Coffee 69
30. Danish Coffee 71
31. Irish coffee Shooter Milkshake 73
32. Good Old Irish 75
33. Bushmills Irish Coffee 77
34. Strong Irish Coffee 79
35. Creamy Irish Coffee 81
36. Old Fashioned Irish Coffee 83
37. Lattetini 85

MOCHA 87

38. Iced Mocha Cappuccino 88
39. Original Iced Coffee 90
40. Mocha Flavored Coffee 92
41. Spicy Mexican Mocha 94
42. Chocolate Coffee 96
43. Peppermint Mocha Coffee 98
44. Mocha Italian Espresso 100
45. Chocolata Coffees 102
46. Chocolate Amaretto Coffee 104
47. Chocolate Mint Coffee Float 106
48. Cocoa Coffee 108
49. Cocoa Hazelnut Mocha 110
50. Chocolate Mint Coffee 112
51. Cafe Au Lait 114
52. Italian Coffee with Chocolate 116
53. Semi Sweet Mocha 118

SPICED COFFEE 120

54. ORANGE SPICE COFFEE 121
55. SPICED COFFEE CREAMER 123
56. CARDAMOM SPICED COFFEE 125
57. CAFE DE OLA 127
58. VANILLA ALMOND COFFEE 129
59. ARABIAN JAVA 131
60. HONEY COFFEE 133
61. CAFE VIENNA DESIRE 135
62. CINNAMON SPICED COFFEE 137
63. CINNAMON ESPRESSO 139
64. MEXICAN SPICED COFFEE 141
65. VIETNAMESE EGG COFFEE 143
66. TURKISH COFFEE 145
67. PUMPKIN SPICED LATTES 148
68. CARAMEL LATTE 151

FRAPPUCCINO AND CAPPUCCINO 153

69. CARAMEL FRAPPUCCINO 154
70. RASPBERRY FRAPPUCCINO 156
71. COFFEE MILK SHAKE 158
72. MOCHA FRAPPE 160
73. INSTANT CARAMEL FRAPPUCCINO 162
74. MANGO FRAPPE 164
75. CAFE CAPPUCCINO 166
76. CAPPUCCINO SHAKE 168
77. CREAMY CAPPUCCINO 170
78. FROZEN CAPPUCCINO 172

FRUITY COFFEE 174

79. RASPBERRY COFFEE 175
80. CHRISTMAS COFFEE 177
81. RICH COCONUT COFFEE 179
82. CHOCOLATE BANANA COFFEE 181

83. Black Forest Coffee 183
84. Maraschino Coffee 185
85. Chocolate Almond Coffee 187
86. Coffee Soda Pop 189
87. Viennese Coffee 191
88. Espresso Romano 193

COFFEE MIXES 195

89. Cafe Au Lait 196
90. Instant Orange Cappuccino 198
91. Swiss Style Mocha Mix 200
92. Instant Creamed Irish Coffee 202
93. Mocha Coffee Mix 204
94. Mocha Instant Coffee 206
95. Viennese Coffee Mix 208
96. Nightcap Coffee Mix 210
97. Cappuccino Mix 212
98. Cafe Cappuccino Mix 214
99. Louisiana Cafe with Milk 216
100. West Indies Coffee 218

CONCLUSION 220

INTRODUCTION

Why do we love coffee so much? Well, apart from the fact that it's super delicious!

A steaming cup of coffee is the first thing millions of people reach for every morning and there are a multitude of reasons these people do so on a daily basis. The caffeine in it plays two roles in why people drink coffee. First, the caffeine in coffee helps to get people' blood moving and makes them feel energized. Early morning workers tend to rely on their coffee to help them get through their work day.

The other reason caffeine is a reason that people drink coffee is that it is addictive. There are many chemicals in coffee that lend to its addictive properties and caffeine is the main one. Caffeine withdrawal can cause headaches and irritability and many people prefer not to give up their coffee.

Coffee has become a very social drink similar in popularity to alcohol. Mornings at the local coffee shop are the place to hang out with friends or meet to discuss business. People tend to drink coffee at these gatherings whether or not they like it which eventually helps them to develop a taste for it and then it becomes addictive.

Coffee drinkers say they drink coffee to relax. While this may seem like an oxymoron considering that coffee is a stimulant, a hot cup of decaffeinated coffee or, for some people, even regular coffee can relax the senses and help them wind down and calm their nerves. Researchers attribute the calming effect to the stimulation of the senses which aids in creativity and mental stimulus which in turn helps calm some people down.

ICED COFFEE

1. Iced Mochacchino

Ingredients:
- 1/2 cup Brewed espresso, chilled
- 6 Tablespoons Chocolate syrup
- 1 Tablespoons Sugar
- 1/2 cup Milk
- 1 cup Vanilla ice cream or frozen yogurt
- 1/4 cup Heavy cream, softly whipped

Directions
a) Place the espresso, chocolate syrup, sugar and milk in a blender, and blend to combine.
b) Add the ice cream or yogurt, and blend until smooth.
c) Pour mixture into two chilled glasses, and top each with whipped cream and chocolate curls or a dusting of the cinnamon or cocoa.

2. Almond Iced Coffee

Ingredients:
- 1 cup strong brewed coffee
- 1 cup skim milk
- 1/2 tsp vanilla extract
- 1/2 tsp almond extract
- 1 tsp of sugar
- Cinnamon for garnish
- Dessert topping

Directions

a) Combine 1 cup strong brewed coffee with 1 cup of skim milk the vanilla extract, almond extract and the sugar.
b) Pour into 2 - 10 ounce iced filled glasses
c) Garnish with the cinnamon.

3. Iced Cinnamon Coffee

Ingredients:
- 4 cup Strong coffee (use 2 to 4 teaspoons instant to 1 cup Boiling water
- 1 3" stick cinnamon, broken in small pieces
- 1/2 cup Heavy cream
- Coffee syrup-syrups come on many flavors. Vanilla would complement the cinnamon.

Directions
a) Pour hot coffee over cinnamon pieces; cover and let stand about 1 hour.
b) Remove cinnamon and stir in cream. Chill thoroughly.
c) To serve, pour into ice-filled glasses. Stir in desired amount of Coffee Syrup.
d) If desired, top with sweetened whipped cream and sprinkle with ground cinnamon. Use cinnamon sticks as stirrers.

4. Coffee Ice

Ingredients:
- 2 cup Brewed espresso
- 1/4 cup Sugar
- 1/2 tsp Ground cinnamon

Directions
a) In a saucepan over medium heat, simmer all ingredients just to dissolve.
b) Place mixture in a metal dish, cover and freeze for at least 5 hours, stirring the outer frozen mixture into the center every half hour, until firm but not solidly frozen.
c) Just before serving, scrape the mixture with a fork to lighten the texture.
Makes 4 (1/2 cup) servings.

5. Iced Cafe Au Lait

Ingredients:
- 2 1/4 Cold Freshly Brewed Coffee
- 2 cups Milk
- 2 Cups Crushed Ice
- Sugar to taste

Directions
a) Blend all ingredients in a blender.
b) Add sugar and continue blending until frothy.
c) Pour over ice
d) Serve immediately.

6. Creamy Iced Coffee

Ingredients:
- 1 cup Chilled Strong Brewed Coffee
- 2 Rounded tablespoons Confectioners' Sugar
- 3 cups Chopped ice

Directions
a) Combine the coffee, sugar and ice
b) Blend until creamy

7. Iced Spiced Coffee

Makes 4 cups

Ingredients

- 1/2 cup coarse ground coffee
- 4 cups room temp water
- 1 cinnamon stick
- 1 whole nutmeg, smashed
- Milk or cream, for serving
- Honey or sugar, for serving

Directions

a) Roughly grind coffee. Use a mallet to lightly smash cinnamon stick and whole nutmeg.
b) In a large container, add coffee and spices and room temperature or slightly warm water. Stir together and Let steep for at least 4 hours or ideally overnight.
c) Strain coffee using a French press or letting it drain through a filter.

d) Pour coffee over ice and add some sweetener and/or cream or milk if you want. It's great black also though!

ALCOHOL-INFUSED COFFEE

8. Rum Coffee

Ingredients:
- 12 oz. Fresh ground coffee, preferably chocolate mint, or Swiss chocolate
- 2 oz. Or more 151 Rum
- 1 Large scoop whipped cream
- 1 oz. Baileys Irish Cream
- 2 Tablespoons Chocolate syrup

Directions
a) Fresh grind the coffee.
b) Brew.
c) In a large mug, put the 2+ oz. of 151 rum in the bottom.
d) Pour the hot coffee into the mug 3/4 of the way up.
e) Add the Bailey's Irish Cream.
f) Stir.
g) Top with the fresh whipped cream and drizzle with the chocolate syrup.

9. Kahlua Irish Coffee

Ingredients:
- 2 oz. Kahlua or coffee liqueur
- 2 oz. Irish Whiskey
- 4 cup Hot coffee
- 1/4 cup Whipping cream, whipped

Directions
a) Pour one-half ounce coffee liqueur in each cup. Add one-half ounce Irish Whiskey to each
b) cup. Pour in steaming freshly-brewed hot coffee, stir. Spoon two heaping
c) tablespoonful of whipped cream on top of each. Serve hot, but not so hot you scorch your lips.

10. Bailey's Irish Cappuccino

Ingredients:
- 3 oz. Bailey's Irish Cream
- 5 oz. Hot coffee -
- Canned dessert topping
- 1 dash Nutmeg

Directions

a) Pour Bailey's Irish Cream into a coffee mug.
b) Fill with hot black coffee. Top with a single spray of dessert topping.
c) Dust dessert topping with a dash of nutmeg

11. Brandy Coffee

Ingredients:
- 3/4 cup Hot Strong Coffee
- 2 ounces of Brandy
- 1 tsp Sugar
- 2 ounces Heavy Cream

Directions

a) Pour the coffee into a tall mug. Add the sugar and stir to dissolve.

b) Add the Brandy and stir again. Pour the cream, over the back of a teaspoon while holding it, slightly above the top of the coffee in the cup. This allows it to float.

c) Serve.

12. Kahlua and chocolate sauce

Ingredients:
- 6 cups Hot coffee
- 1 cup Chocolate syrup
- 1/4 cup Kahlua
- $\frac{1}{8}$ tsp Ground cinnamon
- Whipped cream

Directions
a) Combine coffee, chocolate syrup, Kahlua, and cinnamon in a large container; stir well.
b) Serve immediately. Top with whipped cream.

13. Homemade Coffee Liqueur

Ingredients:
- 4 cup Sugar
- 1/2 cup Instant coffee - use filtered water
- 3 cup Water
- 1/4 tsp Salt
- 1 1/2 cup Vodka, high-proof
- 3 Tablespoons Vanilla

Directions
a) Combine sugar and water; boil till sugar dissolves. Reduce heat to simmer and simmer 1 hour.
b) LET COOL.
c) Stir in vodka and vanilla.

14. Kahlua Brandy Coffee

Ingredients:
- 1 ounce of Kahlua
- 1/2 ounce of Brandy
- 1 cup Hot Coffee
- Whipped Cream for topping

Directions

a) Add Kahlua and brandy to coffee
b) Garnish with the whipped cream

15. Lime Tequila Espresso

Ingredients:
- Double shot of espresso
- 1 shot of White Tequila
- 1 fresh lime

Directions
a) Run a slice of lime around the edge of an espresso glass.
b) Pour a double shot of espresso over ice.
c) Add a single shot of White Tequila
d) Serve

16. Sweetened Brandy Coffee

Ingredients:
- 1 cup Freshly Brewed Coffee
- 1 oz. Coffee Liqueur
- 1tsp Chocolate Syrup
- 1/2 oz. Brandy
- 1 Dash Cinnamon
- Sweet Whipped Cream

Directions

a) Combine coffee liqueur, brandy, chocolate syrup and cinnamon in a mug. Fill with freshly brewed coffee.

b) Top with whipped cream.

17. Dinner Party Coffee

Ingredients:
- 3 cup Very hot decaffeinated Coffee
- 2 Tablespoons Sugar
- 1/4 cup light or dark Rum

Directions
a) Combine very hot coffee, sugar and rum in heated pot.
b) Double as needed.

18. Sweet Maple Coffee

Ingredients:
- 1 cup Half-and-half
- 1/4 cup Maple syrup
- 1 cup Hot brewed coffee
- Sweetened whipped cream

Directions

a) Cook half-and-half and maple syrup in a saucepan over medium heat. Stirring constantly, until thoroughly heated. Do not allow mixture to boil.

b) Stir in coffee, and serve with sweetened whipped cream.

19. Dublin Dream

Ingredients:

- 1Tablespoons Instant coffee
- 1 1/2 Tablespoons Instant hot chocolate
- 1/2 oz. Irish cream liqueur
- 3/4 cup Boiling water
- 1/4 cup Whipped cream

Directions

a) In an Irish coffee glass, place all ingredients except for the whipped cream.
b) Stir until well mixed, and garnish with whipped cream.

20. Di Saronno Coffee

Ingredients:
- 1 oz. Di saronno amaretto
- 8 oz. Coffee
- Whipped cream

Directions
a) Blend Di Saronno Amaretto with coffee, then top with whipped cream.
b) Serve in Irish coffee mug.

21. Baja Coffee

Ingredients:
- 8 cup Hot water
- 3 Tablespoons Instant coffee granules
- 1/2 cup Coffee liqueur
- 1/4 cup Crème de Cacao liqueur
- 3/4 cup Whipped cream
- 2 Tablespoons Semi-sweet chocolate, grated

Directions

a) In slow-cooker, combine hot water, coffee, and liqueurs.
b) Cover and heat on LOW 2-4 hours. Ladle into mugs or heat-proof glasses.
c) Top with whipped cream and grated chocolate.

22. Praline Coffee

Ingredients:
- 3 cups Hot brewed coffee
- 3/4 cups Half-and-half
- 3/4 cups Firmly packed Brown sugar
- 2 Tablespoons Butter or margarine
- 3/4 cup Praline liqueur
- Sweetened whipped cream

Directions

a) Cook first 4 ingredients in a large saucepan over medium heat, stirring constantly, until Thoroughly heated, do not boil.

b) Stir in liqueur; serve with sweetened whipped cream.

23. Praline Liqueur

Ingredients:
- 2 cups Dark Brown Sugar-firmly packed
- 1 cup White Sugar
- 2 1/2 cups of Water
- 4 cups Pecan Pieces
- 4 Vanilla Beans split lengthwise
- 4 cups Vodka

Directions

a) Combine brown sugar, white sugar and water in saucepan over medium heat, until mixture starts to boil. Reduce heat and simmer 5 minutes.

b) Place vanilla beans and pecans into a large glass jar (as this makes 4 1/2 cups Pour hot mixture into jar and let cool. Add vodka

c) Cover tightly and store in a dark place. Turn jar over each day for the next 2 weeks to keep all ingredients combined. After 2 weeks, strain mixture, discarding solids.

24. Amaretto Cafe'

Ingredients:
- 1 1/2 cups Warm Water
- 1/3 cup Amaretto
- 1 Tablespoons Instant Coffee Crystals
- Whipped cream topping

Directions
a) Stir together water and instant coffee crystals in a microwavable dish.
b) Microwave uncovered, on 100% power for about 3 minutes or just till steaming hot.
c) Stir in the Amaretto. Serve in clear glass mugs. Top each mug of coffee mixture with some dessert topping.

25. Cafe Au Cin

Ingredients:
- 1 cup Cold Strong French roast coffee
- 2 Tablespoons Granulated sugar
- dash Cinnamon
- 2 oz. Tawny port
- 1/2 tsp Grated orange peel

Directions

a) Combine and mix in a blender at high speed.
b) Pour into chilled wine glasses.

26. Spiked Cappuccino

Ingredients:
- 1/2 cup Half-and-half
- 1/2 cup Freshly brewed espresso
- 2 Tablespoons Brandy
- 2 Tablespoons White rum
- 2 Tablespoons Dark crème de cacao
- Sugar

Directions

a) Whisk half-and-half in small saucepan over high heat until it becomes frothy, about 3 minutes.
b) Divide espresso coffee between 2 cups. Add half of the brandy and half of the crème de cacao to each cup.
c) Re-whisk half-and-half and pour into cups.
d) Sugar is optional

27. Gaelic Coffee

Ingredients:
- Black coffee; freshly made
- Scotch whiskey
- Raw brown sugar
- Real whipped cream; whipped until slightly thick

Directions
a) Pour the coffee into a warmed glass.
b) Add the whisky and brown sugar to taste. Stir well.
c) Pour some lightly whipped cream into the glass over the back of a teaspoon that is just above the top of the liquid in the cup.
d) It should float a bit.

28. Canadian Coffee

Ingredients:
- 1/4 cup Maple syrup; pure
- 1/2 cup Rye whiskey
- 3 cups Coffee; hot, black, double strength

Topping:
- 3/4 cup of Whipping cream
- 4 tsp Pure Maple syrup

Directions
a) Topping-Whip the 3/4 cup of whipped cream with the 4 tsp of Maple syrup until it forms a soft mound.
b) Divide maple syrup and whiskey among 4 pre-warmed heatproof glass mugs.
c) Pour in coffee to 1 inch from top.
d) Spoon topping over coffee.
e) Serve

29. German Coffee

Ingredients:
- 1/2-ounce cherry brandy
- 5 ounces fresh black coffee
- 1 teaspoon sugar whipped cream
- Maraschino Cherry

Directions
a) Pour the coffee and Cherry brandy into a coffee cup, and add the sugar to sweeten.
b) Top with whipped cream and a maraschino cherry.

30. Danish Coffee

Ingredients:
- 8 c Hot coffee
- 1 c Dark rum
- 3/4 c Sugar
- 2 Cinnamon sticks
- 12 Cloves (whole)

Directions
a) In a very large heavy saucepan, combine all the ingredients, cover and keep on low heat for about 2 hours.
b) Serve in coffee mugs.

31. Irish coffee Shooter Milkshake

Ingredients:
- 1/2 cups Skim milk
- 1/2 cups Plain low-fat yogurt
- 2 tsp Sugar
- 1 tsp Instant coffee powder
- 1 tsp Irish whiskey

Directions
a) Place all ingredients into a blender on low speed.
b) Blend until you can see that your ingredients are incorporated into each other.
c) Use a tall shake glass for presentation.

32. Good Old Irish

Ingredients:
- 1.5 ounces Irish Cream Liqueur
- 1.5 ounces Irish Whiskey
- 1 cup hot brewed coffee
- 1 Tablespoons whipped cream
- 1 dash of nutmeg

Directions
a) In a coffee mug, combine Irish cream and The Irish Whiskey.
b) Fill mug with coffee. Top with a dollop of whipped cream.
c) Garnish with a sprinkle of Nutmeg.

33. Bushmills Irish Coffee

Ingredients:
- 1 1/2 ounces Bushmills Irish whiskey
- 1 tsp Brown sugar (optional)
- 1 dash Crème de menthe, green
- Extra Strong fresh coffee
- Whipped cream

Directions

a) Pour whiskey into Irish coffee cup and fill to 1/2 inch from top with coffee. Add sugar to taste and mix. Top with whipped cream and drizzle crème de menthe on top.

b) Dip rim of cup in sugar to coat edge.

34. Strong Irish Coffee

Ingredients:
- 1 cups of strong Coffee
- 1 1/2 oz. Irish whisky
- 1 tsp Sugar
- 1 Tablespoons Whipped cream

Directions
a) Mix coffee, sugar, and whiskey in a large microwavable mug.
b) Microwave on high 1 to 2 min. Top with whipped cream
c) Careful when drinking, may need a moment to cool.

35. Creamy Irish Coffee

Ingredients:
- 1/3 cup Irish Cream Liqueur
- 1 1/2 cups Freshly Brewed Coffee
- 1/4 cup Heavy Cream, slightly sweetened and whipped

Directions
a) Divide the liqueur and coffee among 2 mugs.
b) Top with whipped cream.
c) Serve.

36. Old Fashioned Irish Coffee

Ingredients:
- 3/4 cup Warm Water
- 2 Tablespoons Irish Whiskey
- Dessert Topping
- 1 1/2 spoons Instant Coffee Crystals
- Brown Sugar to Taste

Directions
a) Combine water and instant coffee crystals. Microwave, uncovered, on
b) 100% power about 1 1/2 minutes or just till steaming hot. Stir in Irish whiskey and brown sugar.

37. Lattetini

Ingredients:
- 1-part Cream Liqueur
- $1\frac{1}{2}$ parts Vodka

Directions
a) Shake with ice and strain into a Martini glass.
b) Enjoy

MOCHA

38. Iced Mocha Cappuccino

Ingredients:
- 1 Tablespoons Chocolate syrup
- 1 cup Hot double espresso or very strong coffee
- 1/4 cup Half-and-half
- 4 Ice cubes

Directions

a) Stir the chocolate syrup into the hot coffee until melted. In a blender, combine the coffee with the half-and-half and the ice cubes.
b) Blend at high speed for 2 to 3 minutes.
c) Serve immediately in a tall, cold glass.

39. Original Iced Coffee

Ingredients:
- 1/4 cup Coffee; instant, regular or decaffeinated
- 1/4 cup Sugar
- 1 litre or quart of cold Milk

Directions
a) Dissolve instant coffee and sugar in hot water. Stir in 1 litre or quart of cold milk and add ice. For mocha flavor, use chocolate milk and add sugar to taste.
b) Dissolve 1 Tablespoon of instant coffee and 2 tsp sugar in 1 Tablespoon hot water.
c) Add 1 cup of cold milk and stir.
d) You can sweeten with a low calorie sweetener instead of sugar

40. Mocha Flavored Coffee

Ingredients:
- 1/4 cup Non-dairy creamer dry
- 1/3 cup Sugar
- 1/4 cup Dry instant coffee
- 2 Tablespoons cocoa

Directions
a) Place all ingredients in mixer, beat at high until well blended. Mix 1 1/2 Tablespoons spoons with a cup of hot water.
b) Store in air tight jar. Such as a canning jar.

41. Spicy Mexican Mocha

Ingredients:
- 6 Ounces Strong Coffee
- 2 Tablespoons Powdered Sugar
- 1 Tablespoons Unsweetened ground chocolate powder
- 1/4 tsp Vietnamese Cassia Cinnamon
- 1/4 tsp Jamaican Allspice
- 1/8 tsp Cayenne Pepper
- 1-3 Tablespoons Heavy Cream or half and half

Directions

a) In a small bowl, mix all dry ingredients together.
b) Pour the coffee in a large mug, stir in the cocoa mix, until smooth.
c) Then add the cream to taste.

42. Chocolate Coffee

Ingredients:
- 2 Tablespoons Instant coffee
- 1/4 cup Sugar
- 1 dash Salt
- 1 oz. Squares unsweetened chocolate
- 1 cup Water
- 3 cup Milk
- Whipped cream

Directions
a) In saucepan combine coffee, sugar, salt, chocolate, and water; stir over low heat until chocolate has melted. Simmer 4 minutes, stirring constantly.
b) Gradually add milk, stirring constantly until heated.
c) When piping hot, remove from heat and beat with rotary beater until mixture is frothy.
d) Pour into cups and sail a dollop of whipped cream on the surface of each.

43. Peppermint Mocha Coffee

Ingredients:
- 6 cups Freshly Brewed Coffee
- 1 1/2 cups of Milk
- 4 ounces of Semi-Sweet Chocolate
- 1 tsp Peppermint Extract
- 8 Peppermint Sticks

Directions
a) Place coffee, milk, chocolate in a large saucepan on low heat for 5-7 minutes or until chocolate has melted, mixture is heated through, stir occasionally.
b) Stir in the peppermint extract
c) Pour into mugs
d) Garnish with a peppermint stick

44. Mocha Italian Espresso

Ingredients:
- 1 cup Instant Coffee
- 1 cup Sugar
- 4 1/2 cups Non Fat Dry Milk
- 1/2 cup Cocoa

Directions
a) Stir all ingredients together.
b) Process in a blender until powdered.
c) Use 2 Tablespoons to one small cup of hot water.
d) Serve in espresso cups
e) Makes about 7 cups of mix
f) Store in a tight fitted lidded jar.
g) Canning jars work well for coffee storage.

45. Chocolata Coffees

Ingredients:
- 1/4 cup Instant espresso
- 1/4 cup Instant cocoa
- 2 cups Boiling water-it's best to use water that has been filtered
- Whipped cream
- Finely shredded orange peel or ground cinnamon

Directions

a) Combine coffee and cocoa. Add boiling water and stir to dissolve. Pour into demitasse cups. Top each serving with whipped cream, shredded orange peel and a dash of cinnamon.

46. Chocolate Amaretto Coffee

Ingredients:
- Amaretto coffee beans
- 1 Tablespoons Vanilla extract
- 1 tsp Almond extract
- 1 tsp Cocoa powder
- 1 tsp Sugar
- Whipped Cream to Garnish

Directions
a) Brew coffee.
b) Add Vanilla and Almond Extract1 tsp cocoa and 1 tsp sugar per cup.
c) Garnish with whipped cream

47. Chocolate Mint Coffee Float

Ingredients:
- 1/2 cup Hot Coffee
- 2 Tablespoons Crème de Cacao Liqueur
- 1 Scoop Mint Chocolate Chip Ice Cream

Directions
a) For each serving combine 1/2 cup coffee and 2 Tablespoon
b) s of the liqueur.
c) Top with a scoop of ice cream.

48. Cocoa Coffee

Ingredients:
- 1/4 cup Powder Non Dairy Creamer
- 1/3 cup Sugar
- 1/4 cup Dry Instant Coffee
- 2 Tablespoons Cocoa

Directions

a) Place all ingredients in a blender, blend on high until well blended.
b) Store in an air tight canning jar.
c) Mix 1 1/2 Tablespoons with 3/4 cup hot water

49. Cocoa Hazelnut Mocha

Ingredients:
- 3/4 oz. Kahlua
- 1/2 cup Hot Hazelnut Coffee
- 1tsp Nestle Quick
- 2 Tablespoons Half and Half

Directions
a) Combine all ingredients in your favorite cu.
b) Stir

50. Chocolate Mint Coffee

Ingredients:
- 1/3 cup Ground Coffee
- 1 tsp Chocolate Extract
- 1/2 tsp Mint Extract
- 1/4 tsp Vanilla Extract

Directions
a) Place coffee in blender.
b) In a cup combine extracts, add extracts to coffee.
c) Process until mixed, just a few seconds.
d) Store refrigerated

51. Cafe Au Lait

Ingredients:
- 2 cup Milk
- 1/2 cup Heavy cream
- 6 cups Louisiana coffee

Directions
a) Combine milk and cream in saucepan; bring just to a boil (bubbles will form around edge of pan), then remove from heat.
b) Pour small amount of coffee in each coffee cup.
c) Pour remaining coffee and hot milk mixture together until cups are about 3/4 full.
d) Skim milk can be substituted for whole milk and cream.

52. Italian Coffee with Chocolate

Ingredients:
- 2 cups Hot Strong Coffee
- 2 cups Hot Traditional Cocoa - try Hershey's brand
- Whipped Cream
- Grated Orange Peel

Directions

a) Combine 1/2 cup coffee and 1/2 cup cocoa in each of the 4 mugs.

b) Top with whipped cream; sprinkle with grated orange peel.

53. Semi Sweet Mocha

Ingredients:
- 4 oz. Semisweet Chocolate
- 1 Tablespoons Sugar
- 1/4 cup Whipping Cream
- 4 cup Hot Strong Coffee
- Whipped Cream
- Grated Orange Peel

Directions

a) Melt chocolate in a heavy saucepan over low heat.
b) Stir in sugar and whipping cream.
c) Beat in coffee using a whisk, 1/2 cup at a time; continue until frothy.
d) Top with whipped cream and sprinkle with grated orange peel.

SPICED COFFEE

54. Orange Spice Coffee

Ingredients:
- 1/4 cup Ground coffee
- 1 Tablespoons Grated orange peel
- 1/2 tsp Vanilla extract
- 1 1/2 Cinnamon sticks

Directions
a) Place coffee and orange peel in a blender or food processor.
b) Stop processor long enough to add the vanilla.
c) Process 10 seconds more.
d) Place mixture in a glass pitcher with the cinnamon sticks and refrigerate.

55. Spiced Coffee Creamer

Ingredients:
- 2 cups Nestlé's quick
- 2 cups powdered coffee creamer
- 1/2 cups Powdered sugar
- 3/4 tsp Cinnamon
- 3/4 tsp Nutmeg

Directions
a) Mix all ingredients together and store in an airtight jar.
b) Mix 4 tsp with one cup of hot water

56. Cardamom Spiced Coffee

Ingredients:
- 3/4 cup Ground Coffee
- 2 2/3 cups of Water
- Ground Cardamom
- 1/2 cup Sweetened Condensed milk

Directions
a) Brew coffee in a drip style or percolator coffee maker.
b) Pour into 4 cups.
c) To each serving add a dash of Cardamom and 2 Tablespoons of condensed milk.
d) Stir
e) Serve

57. Cafe de Ola

Ingredients:
- 8 cups of Filtered Water
- 2 small Cinnamon Sticks
- 3 Whole Cloves
- 4 ounces of Dark Brown Sugar
- 1 Square of Semisweet Chocolate or Mexican Chocolate
- 4 ounces Ground Coffee

Directions
a) Bring the water to a boil.
b) Add the cinnamon, cloves, sugar and chocolate.
c) Bring to a boil again, skim off any foam.
d) Reduce the heat to low and DO NOT ALLOW IT TO BOIL
e) Add the coffee and allow steeping for 5 minutes.

58. Vanilla Almond Coffee

Ingredients:
- 1/3 cup ground Coffee
- 1 tsp Vanilla Extract
- 1/2 tsp Almond Extract
- 1/4 tsp Anise Seeds

Directions
a) Place coffee in a blender
b) Combine remaining ingredients in a separate cup
c) Add the extract and seeds to the coffee in the blender
d) Process until combined
e) Use the mixture as usual when brewing coffee
f) Makes 8-6 ounce servings
g) Store unused portion in refrigerator

59. Arabian Java

Ingredients:
- 1 pint of Filtered Water
- 3 Tablespoons of coffee
- 3 Tablespoons of Sugar
- 1/4 tsp of Cinnamon
- 1/4 tsp of Cardamom
- 1 tsp of Vanilla or Vanilla Sugar

Directions
a) Mix all ingredients into a saucepan and heat until foam gathers on top.
b) Do not pass through a filter.
c) Stir before serving

60. Honey Coffee

Ingredients:
- 2 cups Fresh Coffee
- 1/2 cup of Milk
- 4 Tablespoons of Honey
- 1/8 tsp Cinnamon
- Dash Nutmeg or Allspice
- Drop or 2 of Vanilla Extract

Directions
a) Heat ingredients in a saucepan, but do not boil.
b) Stir well to combine ingredients.
c) A delightful dessert coffee.

61. Cafe Vienna Desire

Ingredients:
- 1/2 cup Instant coffee
- 2/3 cup Sugar
- 2/3 cup Non-fat powered milk
- 1/2 tsp Cinnamon
- 1 pinch Cloves -adjust to taste
- 1 pinch Allspice-adjust to taste
- 1 pinch Nutmeg-adjust to taste

Directions

a) Mix all ingredients together
b) Use a blender to blend into a very fine powder. Use 1 tablespoon per mug of hot filtered water.

62. Cinnamon Spiced Coffee

Ingredients:
- 1/3 cup Instant coffee
- 3 Tablespoons Sugar
- 8 Whole cloves
- 3 Inches stick cinnamon
- 3 cup Water
- Whipped cream
- Ground cinnamon

Directions

a) Combine 1/3 cup instant coffee, 3 tablespoons sugar, cloves, stick cinnamon, and water.

b) Cover, bring to boiling. Remove from heat and let stand, covered, about 5 minutes to steep.

c) Strain. Pour into cups and top each with spoonful of whipped cream. Add a dash of cinnamon.

63. Cinnamon Espresso

Ingredients:
- 1 cup Cold water
- 2 Tablespoons Ground espresso coffee
- 1/2 Cinnamon stick (3" long)
- 4 tsp Crème de Cacao
- 2 tsp Brandy
- 2 Tablespoons Whipping cream, chilled
  Grated semisweet chocolate to garnish

Directions

a) Use your espresso machine for this or really strong coffee with a small amount of Filtered water.
b) Break a cinnamon stick into small pieces and add to the hot espresso.
c) Allow to cool 1 minute.
d) Add crème de cacao and brandy, and stir gently. Pour into demitasse
e) Cups. Whip the cream, and float some cream on top of each cup. Garnish with grated Chocolate or chocolate curls.

64. Mexican Spiced Coffee

Ingredients:
- 3/4 cup Brown sugar, firmly packed
- 6 Cloves
- 6 Julienne slices orange zest
- 3 Cinnamon sticks
- 6 Tablespoonssp. Real brewed Coffee

Directions
a) In a large saucepan, heat 6 cups of water with the brown sugar, cinnamon sticks, and cloves over moderately high heat until the mixture is hot, but do not let it boil. Add the coffee, bring the mixture to a boil, stirring occasionally, for 3 minutes.
b) Strain the coffee through a fine sieve and serve in coffee cups with the orange zest.

65. Vietnamese Egg Coffee

Ingredients:
- 1 egg
- 3 teaspoons of Vietnamese coffee powder
- 2 teaspoons of sweetened condensed milk
- Boiling water

Directions

a) Brew a small cup of Vietnamese coffee.

b) Crack an egg and discard the whites.

c) Put the yolk and the sweetened condensed milk in a small, deep bowl and

whisk vigorously until you end up with a frothy, fluffy mixture like the one above.
d) Add a tablespoon of the brewed coffee and whisk it in.
e) In a clear coffee cup pour in your brewed coffee, and then add the fluffy egg mixture on top.

66. Turkish Coffee

Ingredients:
- 3/4 cup Water
- 1 Tablespoons Sugar
- 1 Tablespoons Pulverized Coffee
- 1 Cardamom Pod

Directions
a) Bring water and sugar to a boil.
b) Remove from heat-add coffee and cardamom
c) Stir well and return to heat.
d) When coffee foams up, remove from heat and let grounds settle.
e) Repeat twice more. Pour into cups.
f) The coffee grounds should settle before drinking.
g) You can serve the coffee with the cardamom pod in the cup-your choice

Turkish Coffee Tips

h) Must always be served with foam on top
i) You can request that your coffee be ground for Turkish Coffee-it is a powder consistency.
j) Do not stir after pouring into cups as the foam will collapse

k) Always use cold water when preparing
l) Cream or milk is never added to Turkish Coffee; however, sugar is optional

67. Pumpkin Spiced Lattes

Ingredients:
- 2 tablespoons canned pumpkin
- 1/2 teaspoon pumpkin pie spice, plus more to garnish
- Freshly ground black pepper
- 2 tablespoons sugar
- 2 tablespoons pure vanilla extract
- 2 cups whole milk
- 1 to 2 shots espresso, about 1/4 cup
- 1/4 cup heavy cream, whipped until firm peaks form

Directions

a) Heat the pumpkin and spices: In a small saucepan over medium heat cook the pumpkin with the pumpkin pie spice and a generous helping of black pepper for 2 minutes or until it's hot and smells cooked. Stir constantly.

b) Add the sugar and stir until the mixture looks like a bubbly thick syrup.

c) Whisk in the milk and vanilla extract. Warm gently over medium heat, watching carefully to make sure it doesn't boil over.

d) Carefully process the milk mixture with a hand blender or in a traditional blender (hold the lid down tightly with a thick wad of towels!) until frothy and blended.
e) Mix the drinks: Make the espresso or coffee and divide between two mugs and add the frothed milk.
f) Top with whipped cream and a sprinkle of pumpkin pie spice, cinnamon, or nutmeg if desired.

68. Caramel Latte

Ingredients:
- 2 ounces espresso
- 10 ounces milk
- 2 tablespoons home-made caramel sauce plus more for drizzling
- 1 tablespoon sugar (optional)

Directions
a) Pour the espresso into a mug.
b) Place the milk in a wide glass or glass jar and microwave for 30 seconds until it is very hot but not boiling.
c) Alternatively, heat the milk in a saucepan over medium heat for about 5 minutes until very hot but not boiling, watching it carefully.
d) Add the caramel sauce and sugar (if using) to the hot milk and stir until they dissolve.
e) Using a milk frother, froth the milk until you don't see any bubbles and you have a thick froth, 20 to 30 seconds. Swirl the glass and lightly tap it on the counter repeatedly to pop the larger bubbles. Repeat this step as needed.
f) Using a spoon to hold back the foam, pour the milk into the espresso. Spoon the remaining foam on top.

FRAPPUCCINO AND CAPPUCINO

69. Caramel Frappuccino

Ingredients:
- 1/2 cup of cold coffee
- 3 Tablespoons of sugar
- 1/2 cup of milk
- 2 cups of ice
- Whipped Cream-use the canned kind that you can squirt on top
- 3 Tablespoons of caramel sundae sauce

Directions
a) Combine all ingredients in a blender
b) Blend drink until ice is crushed and drink is smooth
c) Serve in chilled coffee mugs with whipped cream and the caramel sauce drizzled on top.

70. Raspberry Frappuccino

Ingredients:
- 2 cups crushed ice cubes
- 1 1/4 cups-extra strong brewed coffee
- 1/2 cup of milk
- 2 Tablespoons vanilla or raspberry syrup
- 3 Tablespoons chocolate syrup
- Whipped Cream

Directions
a) Combine ice cubes, coffee, milk and syrups in a blender.
b) Blend until nicely smooth.
c) Pour into chilled tall serving mugs or soda fountain glasses.
d) Top with whipped cream, drizzle chocolate and raspberry syrup on top.
e) Add a maraschino cherry if desired

71. Coffee Milk Shake

Ingredients:
- 2 cup Milk
- 2 Tablespoons Sugar
- 2 tsp Instant coffee
- 3 Tablespoons Vanilla ice cream
- Strong coffee that is cold

Directions

a) Add all ingredients in blender in order given and mix at high speed until blended.

b) Serve in soda fountain glasses.

72. Mocha Frappe

Ingredients:
- 18 Ice cubes (up to 22)
- 7 oz. Double strength coffee, chilled
- 1/2 cup Chocolate sauce (or syrup)
- 2 Tablespoons Vanilla Syrup
- Whipped Cream

Directions
a) Use a blender.
b) Place ice, coffee, chocolate sauce, and syrup in the blender. Blend until smooth. Pour into a large, tall, chilled, soda fountain glass.
c) Garnish with dollop of whipped cream or scoop of ice cream.

73. Instant Caramel Frappuccino

Ingredients:
- 1/3 glass of ice
- 1/3 glass of milk
- 1 Tablespoon instant coffee
- 2 Tablespoons caramel syrup

Directions
a) Mix all the ingredients together in a blender until the ice is nicely crushed and the milk frothy.
b) Serve immediately.

74. Mango Frappe

Ingredients:
- 1 1/2 cups of Mango, cut up
- 4-6 Ice Cubes
- 1 cup of milk
- 1 Tablespoons Lemon Juice
- 2 Tablespoons of sugar
- 1/4 tsp of Vanilla Extract

Directions

a) Place the cut Mango into the freezer for 30 minutes
b) Combine Mango, milk, sugar, lemon juice and vanilla in a blender. Blend until smooth.
c) Add ice cubes and process until cubes are smooth as well.
d) Serve immediately.

75. Cafe Cappuccino

Ingredients:
- 1/2 cup Instant Coffee
- 3/4 cup Sugar
- 1 cup Non Fat Dry Milk
- 1/2 tsp Dried Orange Peel

Directions
a) Crush dried orange peel in mortar and pestle
b) Use 2 tablespoons for each cup of hot water

76. Cappuccino Shake

Ingredients:
- 1 cup Skim Milk
- 1 1/2 tsp of Instant Coffee
- 2 packages of artificial sweetener
- 1/4 of an ounce of Brandy or Rum Flavoring
- 1 Dash of Cinnamon

Directions

a) In a blender combine milk, coffee, sweetener and Brandy or rum extract.
b) Blend until coffee is dissolved.
c) Serve with a dash of cinnamon.
d) For a hot drink, warm on the microwave.

77. Creamy Cappuccino

Ingredients:
- 1/4 cup Instant Espresso or Instant Dark Roast Coffee
- 2 cups Boiling Water
- 1/2 cup Heavy Cream, whipped
- Cinnamon, Nutmeg, or finely shredded Orange Peel
- Sugar

Directions

a) Dissolve coffee in boiling water, Pour into small, tall cups.
b) Filling only half way.

Add a dash of:

a) Cinnamon, Nutmeg, or finely shredded Orange Peel
b) Fold the cream into the coffee.

78. Frozen Cappuccino

Ingredients:
- 2 scoops of Vanilla Frozen Yogurt- Divided
- 1/2 cup Milk
- 1 Tablespoons of Hershey's Chocolate Powder
- 1 1/2 tsp Instant Coffee Granules

Directions
a) Place 1 scoop of the frozen yogurt, the milk, chocolate powder, and coffee granules in a food processor or blender.
b) Process 30 seconds or until smooth.
c) Pour into a tall soda fountain glass.
d) Top with remaining scoop of yoghurt.

FRUITY COFFEE

79. Raspberry Coffee

Ingredients:
- 1/4 cup of Brown Sugar
- Coffee grounds for a 6 cup pot of regular coffee
- 2 tsp of Raspberry Extract

Directions
a) Place raspberry extract into the empty coffee pot
b) Place brown sugar and coffee grounds in coffee filter
c) Add the 6 cups of water to the top and brew the pot.

80. Christmas Coffee

Ingredients:
- 1 pot of coffee (10-cup equivalent)
- 1/2 cup sugar
- 1/3 cup water
- 1/4 cup unsweetened cocoa
- 1/4 teaspoon cinnamon
- 1 pinch grated nutmeg
- Whipping cream for topping

Directions

a) Prepare pot of coffee.
b) In a medium sauce pan, heat water to a low boil. Add sugar, cocoa, cinnamon and nutmeg.
c) Bring back to a low boil for about a minute - stirring occasionally.
d) Combine coffee and cocoa/spice mixture and serve topped with whipped cream.

81. Rich Coconut Coffee

Ingredients:
- 2 cups Half-and-half
- 15 oz. Can cream of coconut
- 4 cups Hot brewed coffee
- Sweetened whipped cream

Directions
a) Bring half-and-half and cream of coconut to a boil in a saucepan over medium heat, stirring constantly.
b) Stir in coffee.
c) Serve with sweetened whipped cream.

82. Chocolate Banana Coffee

Ingredients:
- Make a 12 cup pot of your regular coffee
- Add 1/2-1 tsp of Banana Extract
- Add 1-1 1/2 tsp of cocoa

Directions
a) Combine
b) So simple...and perfect for a house full of guests

83. Black Forest Coffee

Ingredients:
- 6 oz. Fresh brewed coffee
- 2 Tablespoons Chocolate syrup
- 1 Tablespoons Maraschino cherry juice
- Whipped cream
- Shaved chocolate
- Maraschino cherries

Directions
a) Combine coffee, the chocolate syrup, and cherry juice in a cup. Mix well.
b) Top with whipped cream the chocolate shavings and a cherry or 2.

84. Maraschino Coffee

Ingredients:
- 1 cup of Black coffee
- 1 oz. Amaretto
- Whipped topping
- 1 Maraschino cherry

Directions
a) Fill coffee mug or cup with hot black coffee. Stir in the amaretto.
b) Top with whipped topping and a cherry.

85. Chocolate Almond Coffee

Ingredients:
- 1/3 cup Ground coffee
- 1/4 tsp Freshly ground nutmeg
- 1/2 tsp Chocolate extract
- 1/2 tsp Almond extract
- 1/4 cup Toasted almonds, chopped

Directions

a) Process nutmeg and coffee, add extracts. Process 10 seconds longer. Place in bowl and stir in almonds. Store in refrigerator.

b) Makes 8 six ounce servings. To brew: Place mix in filter of an automatic drip coffee maker.

c) Add 6 cups water and brew

86. Coffee Soda Pop

Ingredients:
- 3 cup Chilled double-strength coffee
- 1 Tablespoons Sugar
- 1 cup Half and half
- 4 Scoops (1 pint) coffee ice cream
- 3/4 cup Chilled club soda
- Sweetened whipped cream
- 4 Maraschino cherries,
- Garnish-chocolate curls or cocoa

Directions

a) Combine the coffee and sugar blend in the half and half.
b) Fill 4 tall soda glasses halfway with the coffee mixture
c) Add a scoop of ice cream and fill the glasses to the top with the soda.
d) Garnish with the whipped cream, chocolate or cocoa.
e) Great treat for parties
f) Use a decaf for parties with youngsters

87. Viennese Coffee

Ingredients:
- 2/3 cup dry instant coffee
- 2/3 cup sugar
- 3/4 cup powdered non-dairy creamer
- 1/2 tsp cinnamon
- Dash each of ground allspice, cloves, and nutmeg.

Directions
a) Mix all ingredients together and Store in air tight jar.
b) Mix 4 tsp with one cup hot water.
c) This makes a wonderful gift.
d) Place all ingredients in a canning jar.
e) Decorate with a ribbon and hang tag.
f) The hang tag should have the mixing instructions typewritten on it.

88. Espresso Romano

Ingredients:
- 1/4 cup Fine Ground Coffee
- 1 1/2 cups Cold Water
- 2 strips of Lemon Peel

Directions
a) Place ground coffee in the filter of a drip coffee pot
b) Add water and brew according to machine brewing instructions
c) Add lemon to each cup
d) Serve

COFFEE MIXES

89. Cafe Au Lait

Ingredients:
- 1 cups Milk
- 1 cups Light cream
- 3 Tablespoons Instant coffee
- 2 cups Boiling water

Directions

a) Over low heat, heat milk and cream until hot. Meanwhile, dissolve coffee in Boiling water. Before serving, beat milk mixture with rotary beater-till foamy. Pour milk Mixture into warmed pitcher, and coffee in a separate pitcher.

b) To serve: Fill cups by pouring from both pitchers at the same time, making the streams meet as you pour.

c) This coffee makes a wonderful presentation as well as delicious favor.

90. Instant Orange Cappuccino

Ingredients:
- 1/3 cup Powdered non-dairy creamer
- 1/3 cup Sugar
- 1/4 Dry instant coffee
- 1 or 2 orange hard candies (crushed)

Directions
a) Blend all ingredients together in mixer.
b) Mix 1 Tablespoons with 3/4 cup hot water.
c) Store in airtight jar.

91. Swiss Style Mocha Mix

Ingredients:
- 1/2 cup Instant coffee granules
- 1/2 cup Sugar
- 2 Tablespoons Cocoa
- 1 cup Nonfat dry milk powder

Directions
a) Combine all and mix well. Store mix in an airtight container.
b) For each serving:
c) Place 1 Tablespoon + 1 tsp. of mix into a cup.
d) Add 1 cup boiling water and stir well.

92. Instant Creamed Irish Coffee

Ingredients:
- 1 1/2 Cup Warm Water
- 1 Tablespoons Instant Coffee Crystals
- 1/4 cup Irish Whiskey
- Brown Sugar to Taste
- Whipped Topping

Directions

a) In a 2-cup measure combine water and instant coffee crystals. Microwave, uncovered, on 100% power about 4 minutes or just till steaming.

b) Stir in Irish whiskey and brown sugar. Serve in mugs.

c) Top each mug with whipped topping.

93. Mocha Coffee Mix

Ingredients:
- 1/4 cup Powdered non-dairy creamer
- 1/3 cup Sugar
- 1/4 cup Dry instant coffee
- 2 Tablespoons. Cocoa

Directions
a) Place all ingredients in mixer, beat at high until well blended. Mix 1 1/2 Tablespoons
b) with a cup of hot water.
c) Store in airtight jar. Such as a canning jar.

94. Mocha Instant Coffee

Ingredients:
- 1 cup Instant coffee crystals
- 1 cup Hot chocolate or cocoa mix
- 1 cup Non-dairy creamer
- 1/2 cup Sugar

Directions

a) Combine all ingredients; mix thoroughly. Store in a tightly- covered jar. Try a canning jar.
b) To serve: Place 1 1/2 - 2 tablespoons into a cup or mug.
c) Stir in boiling water to fill cup.
d) Makes 3 1/2 cups coffee mix or about 25 or more servings.

95. Viennese Coffee Mix

Ingredients:
- 2/3 cup (scant) dry instant coffee
- 2/3 cup Sugar
- 3/4 cup Powdered non-dairy creamer
- 1/2 tsp Cinnamon
- dash Ground allspice
- dash Cloves
- dash Nutmeg

Directions
a) Mix all ingredients and store in airtight jar.
b) Mix 4 tsp with 1 cup hot water.

96. Nightcap Coffee Mix

Ingredients:
- 2/3 cup Nondairy coffee creamer
- 1/3 cup Instant Decaf coffee granules
- 1/3 cup Granulated sugar
- 1 tsp Ground cardamom
- 1/2 tsp Ground cinnamon

Directions

a) Combine all ingredients in a medium bowl; stir until well blended.
b) Store in airtight container. Yields 1 1/3 cups coffee mix
c) Spoon 1 heaping tablespoon coffee mix into 8 ounces hot water. Stir until well blended.

97. Cappuccino Mix

Ingredients:
- 6 tsp Instant coffee
- 4 Tablespoons Unsweetened cocoa
- 1 tsp Ground cinnamon
- 5 Tablespoons Sugar
- Whipped cream

Directions
a) Mix all ingredients.
b) To make one serving of coffee use 1 tablespoon of mixture and place in large mug; pour $1 \frac{1}{2}$ cups boiling water over and stir.
c) Top with whipped cream

98. Cafe Cappuccino Mix

Ingredients:
- 1/2 cup Instant coffee
- 3/4 cup Sugar
- 1 cup of Nonfat dry milk
- 1/2 tsp Dried orange peel

Directions
a) Grind the dried orange peel with a mortar and pestle. Stir together all ingredients.
b) Use a blender to combine, until powdered.
c) For each serving:
d) Use 2 Tablespoons for each cup of hot water.
e) Makes about 2 1/4 cups of mix.

99. Louisiana Cafe with Milk

Ingredients:
- 2 cups Milk
- Sugar
- 1 cup Louisiana coffee

Directions
a) Put milk in saucepan; bring to a boil.
b) Pour hot freshly brewed coffee and milk simultaneously into cups; sweeten with sugar to taste.

100. West Indies Coffee

Ingredients:
- 3 1/2 cups Whole Milk
- 1/4 cup Instant coffee
- 1/4 cup Brown sugar
- 1 dash Salt

Directions
a) Place the instant coffee, brown sugar and salt in your mug.
b) Bring milk carefully to just beginning to boil. Stir to dissolve.
c) Serve in heavy mugs.
d) Makes 4 servings.

CONCLUSION

There are millions of people who simply love the taste of coffee. This taste is different for every coffee drinker because of the vast variety of coffee flavors, roasts and varieties available on the market. Some people like a deep dark coffee flavor while other people like a lighter roast that is smooth and mellow.

Regardless of the flavor, people are enticed to their morning cup of coffee. The top reasons people drink coffee is as varied as the types of coffee available to drink. Regardless of the reasons why people drink coffee it is second only to water in consumption and every day the number of coffee drinkers grow tremendously adding their own reasons for drinking it to the list.

If you are a coffee enthusiast or a new convert, this cookbook will go a long way to deepening your love for coffee!

Happy Brewing!

www.ingramcontent.com/pod-product-compliance
Lightning Source LLC
Chambersburg PA
CBHW070406120526
44590CB00014B/1281